JESUS TAUGHT US TO PRAY
THE LORD'S PRAYER

By **David Clark**

Illustrations by **Lisa Ryan**

Copyright © 2016 by YWAM Minneapolis
This book may not be reproduced in whole or in part, by any means, without permission.
For information contact:
YWAM Minneapolis
PO Box 268
Rockford, MN 55373

Printed in China

Hi there! My name is Abby. I'm a follower of Jesus and I love talking about all the things that I've learned from him.

Jesus loves to pray, and when he prays something exciting always seems to happen.

I remember the day that he was baptized. As he prayed, the Father spoke to him from heaven saying, "You're my son and I love you." And then the Holy Spirit came fluttering down on him like a beautiful white dove!

He told us about another time when he went out to pray in the hot, sandy desert for forty days! The Devil tried to make him do bad things, but Jesus just told him "Go away!" and the Devil had to leave.

And then there was the day that he was praying on top of a mountain. His face began to shine like the sun and his clothes became white as snow. He was so beautiful!

When we saw all of these things happening, we decided that we wanted to learn how to pray just like Jesus. So my dad and some of his friends asked him, and Jesus taught us a special prayer that we call the Lord's Prayer. I say it all the time with my family and my church.

Would you like to learn how to pray the Lord's Prayer with me?

Great! Maybe you've heard this before.
First we say: "Our Father in heaven, hallowed be your name."

We call him "Our Father" because he loves us and will always take care of us.

We say that he is "in heaven" because he is the one and only true God.

To "hallow" something means to treat it like its special. We say "hallowed be your name," because we want everybody in the world to treat the name of Jesus in a special way. We want them to love him, praise him, and do the things that make him happy.

Can you think of some things that make Jesus happy?

The next part of the Lord's Prayer says: "Your kingdom come."

Jesus is the king, and someday this whole world will be his kingdom.

We ask him to change this world by taking away the bad things and by making it a place where everyone loves one another.

Next we say, "Your will be done."

God's will is for us to do the right thing.

But sometimes we make mistakes. We fight, we're mean, and we don't want to share.

We ask God to change our hearts, so that we can always do what is right.

Heaven is the place where everything is perfect and beautiful. Everyone there loves God and obeys him. We want this earth to be like that too. So we ask God to change the world, and make it just like heaven.

Let's say together what we've learned so far.

Our Father in heaven,
hallowed be your name.
Your kingdom come.
Your will be done,
on earth as it is in heaven.

You did a great job!

Now the rest of the prayer goes like this:

"Give us today our daily bread."

Here we ask God to give us all the things we need like food, clothes, a bed to sleep in, and even toys to play with. We are also promising God that we will share what we have with other people.

What are some things we have that we can share with others?

Next we say, "And forgive us our sins, as we forgive those who sin against us."

We say sorry to God for the naughty things we've done. But we also tell him that we have decided to love and forgive all the people that have hurt our feelings.

Is there anybody that you need to forgive?

Then the Lord's Prayer says: "Lead us not into temptation, but deliver us from evil."

Temptation happens when we think about doing something bad. The evil one is the Devil, and he tries to trick us.

We ask God to help us say "No!" to the bad things that the Devil wants us to do.

And because we know that God is stronger than the evil one, we ask him to protect us when the Devil tries to do us harm.

We end the Lord's Prayer by saying: "For yours is the kingdom, and the power, and the glory, forever and ever. Amen."

This is our special way of praising God and thanking him for answering our prayers.

Are you ready to say the whole thing?

Our Father in heaven,
hallowed be your name.
Your kingdom come.
Your will be done,
on earth as it is in heaven.
Give us today our daily bread.
And forgive us our sins,
as we forgive those who sin against us.
Lead us not into temptation.
But deliver us from evil.
For yours is the kingdom,
and the power,
and the glory,
forever and ever,
Amen.

You did it! Good job!
Now you can pray just like Jesus!

The Lord's Prayer is the perfect prayer,
because Jesus is the perfect teacher.

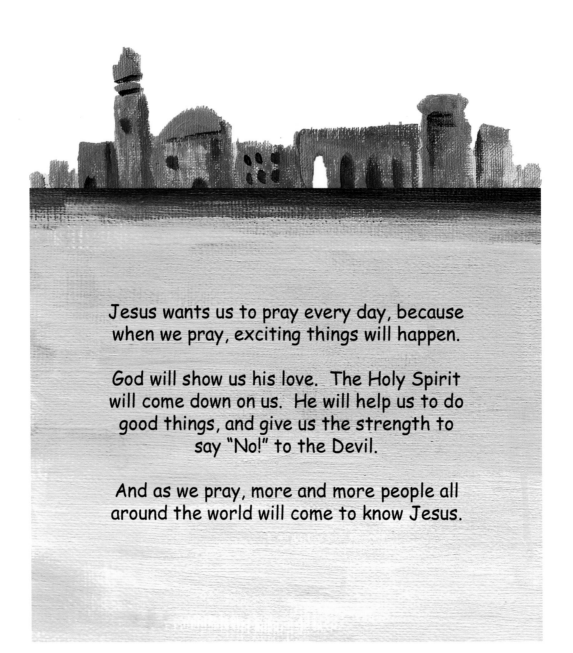

Jesus wants us to pray every day, because when we pray, exciting things will happen.

God will show us his love. The Holy Spirit will come down on us. He will help us to do good things, and give us the strength to say "No!" to the Devil.

And as we pray, more and more people all around the world will come to know Jesus.

I hope you have fun praying the Lord's Prayer.
Exciting things will be happening soon!

Parents:

My translation of the Lord's Prayer is an integration of Matt 6:9-10 and Luke 11:2-4. Different churches say this prayer in a variety of ways. Feel free to adapt the words according to the way it is spoken in your family's tradition.

Notes on the Lord's Prayer:

- "Our Father in Heaven": See Psalm 115: 2-8. Note the contrast between the false gods on the earth and the true God who is "in heaven" (vs 3).

- "Hallowed be your Name": Alternative translations are: "May your name be honored as holy," or "Show the greatness of your name." This is a petition for God's reputation on earth to be honorable.

- "Your Kingdom Come": The kingdom of which Jesus spoke is the same kingdom for which David prayed in Psalm 72.

- "Your will be done": The Father's will is done when people do the things that please him. In the Gospels, it's all about putting into practice the teachings of Jesus (see Matt 7:21; 12:50; 21:31).

- "On earth as it is in heaven": The first section of the Lord's Prayer focuses on the Father in heaven. The second section focuses on the needs of humanity on earth.

- "Give us this day our daily bread": This petition hearkens back to the giving of the manna (Ex. 16:14-21).

- "Forgive us our sins as we forgive those who sin against us": Matthew's version of the Lord's Prayer utilizes the Aramaic idea of "debts". Luke refers to both sin and debt.

- "Lead us not into temptation": See Luke 22:40, 46, where Jesus tells his disciples: "Pray that you may not enter into temptation."

- "Deliver us from evil." The translation can be "evil" or "the evil one."

- "For yours is the kingdom and the power and the glory" is not found in Luke's version of the Lord's Prayer, nor in the oldest manuscripts of Matthew. But there is ample evidence that many early churches ended the Lord's Prayer in this way.

If you have questions or comments about the Lord's Prayer, or are interested in finding additional resources, please visit www.amazon.com/author/daclark

Autobiographical Notes from the Author:

I grew up in a church that said the Lord's Prayer every Sunday, but as a child I had little appreciation for its value. As my personal relationship with Christ deepened during my youth, prayer itself became increasingly important to me. It seemed that the more I prayed, the more God responded. Seeing his hand at work in the lives of those around me, and in my own life, I became increasingly excited about the possibilities that the Lord opened to me through prayer.

My passion over the years has been not only to pray, but to understand the theology of prayer. This pursuit ultimately led to a PhD on the topic of Lord's Prayer, and two books for "big people." Needless to say I no longer think of this prayer as a boring recitation.

My wife Kim and I are the parents of five children, and as my youngest daughter Elisabeth grows, I long to teach her the power of this prayer. That desire became the inspiration for this book. My hope is that this small tome will help you, and the little ones in your own life discover anew the awesome power of the greatest prayer the world has ever known!

About the Illustrator:

Lisa Ryan published her first illustrated work on stapled printer paper at age four and has considered herself an artist ever since. Known for her whimsical style, Lisa has moved on from the crayons of her childhood and now works predominantly with acrylic. Lisa and her husband Tommy currently reside in Minnesota where they enjoy reading children's books to their daughter and telling her about their best friend Jesus.

The publication of this book was made possible by
Youth With A Mission (YWAM) Minneapolis.
We are a community comprised of people from many nations
and Christian denominations, who are committed to knowing God
and making him known throughout the world.

Our ministries include:
- Discipleship and missionary training schools.
- Mission Adventures: short-term outreaches for church groups.
- Kids Against Hunger: a food packing program that
  sends food to hungry children around the world.
- The Nest: a shelter for pregnant women.
- Impact Minneapolis: community development projects
  throughout the Twin Cities.

If you would like to learn more about our work, or make a contribution,
please visit our website: www.ywam-mn.org